Introductory Calculus For Infants

By Omi M. Inouye

Dedicated to:
Cassandra Zoe Miles

Cassandra, you have a mother who fearlessly dances with fire,
and a father whose work has been buried under the ocean and may soon be
shot into orbit.
There is no limit to what you can learn from them.

This book is for entertainment purposes only.
The author is not a professor and is not qualified to teach anyone anything.

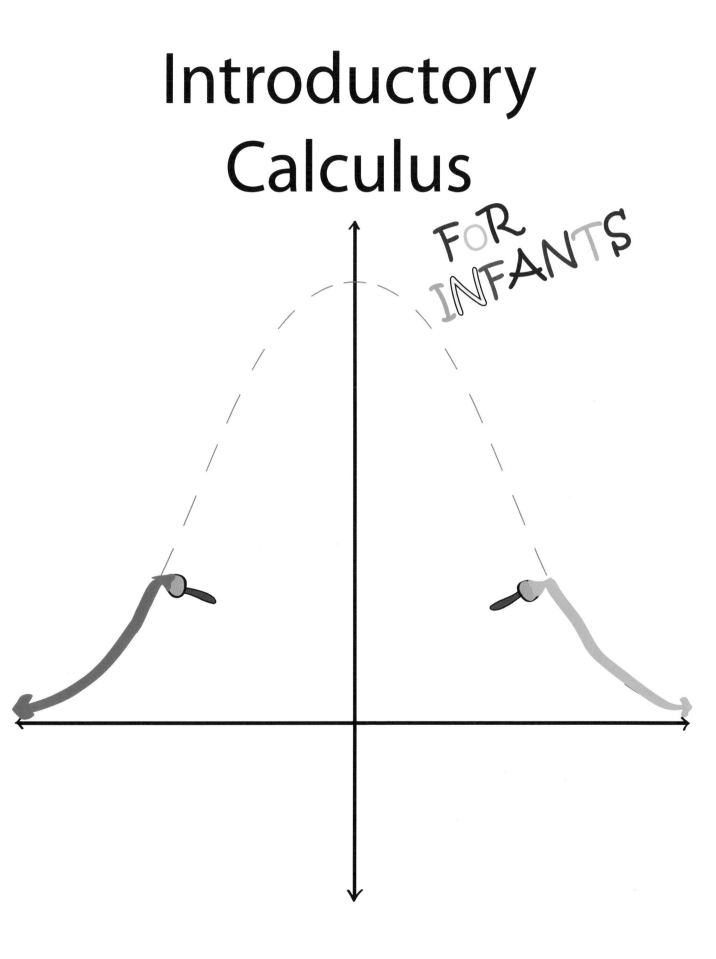

This is a.

Many things start with the letter a.

apple

alien

astronaut

this book

There are lots of other letters...

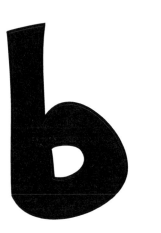

and lots of words start with them too.

etc...

This is x.

Not very many words start with x.

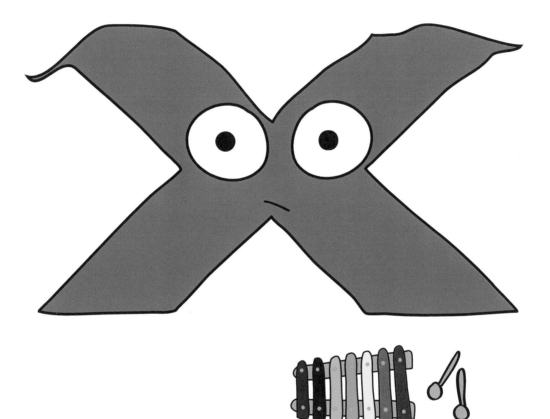

Many of the other letters were mean to him.

You're boring!

Nobody likes you!

This is f.

She is fabulous and fun.

She didn't like the way the other letters treated x.

You're not being very good friends!

One Friday, f went over
to x's house.

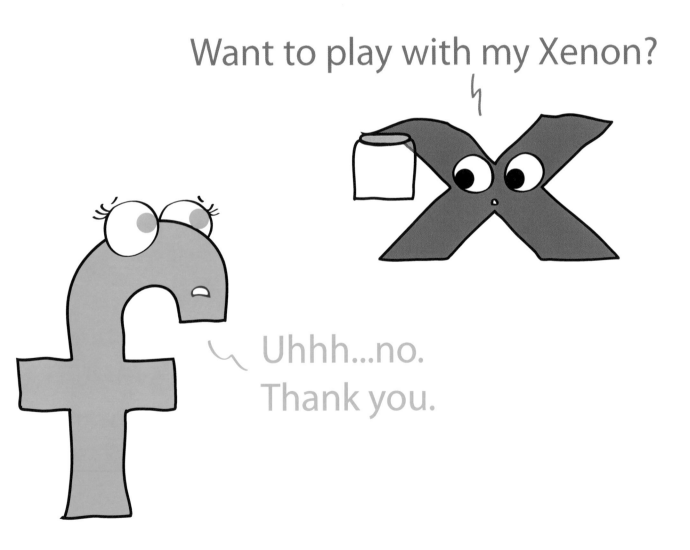

You can be fun if you
want to be!

With me by your side
you can be anything!

You can be Absolute!

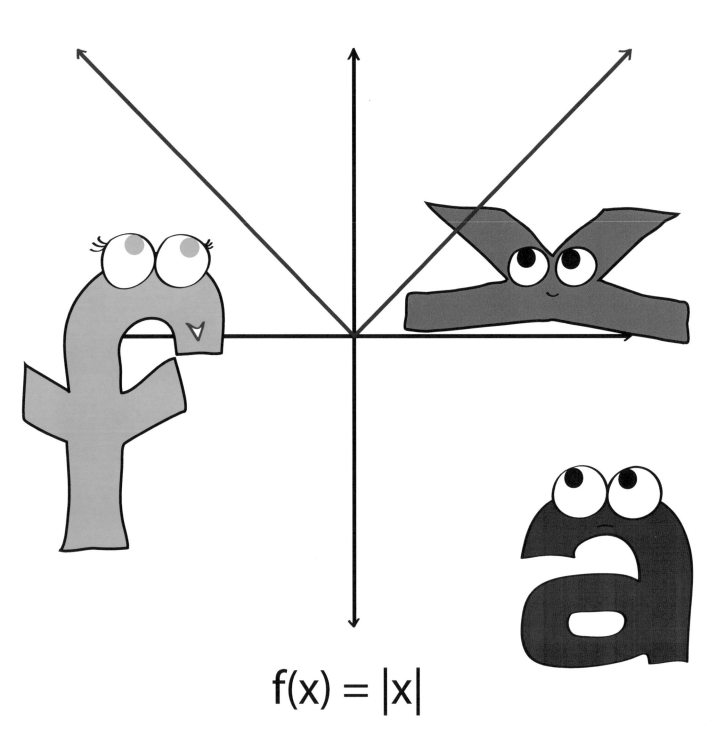

$$f(x) = |x|$$

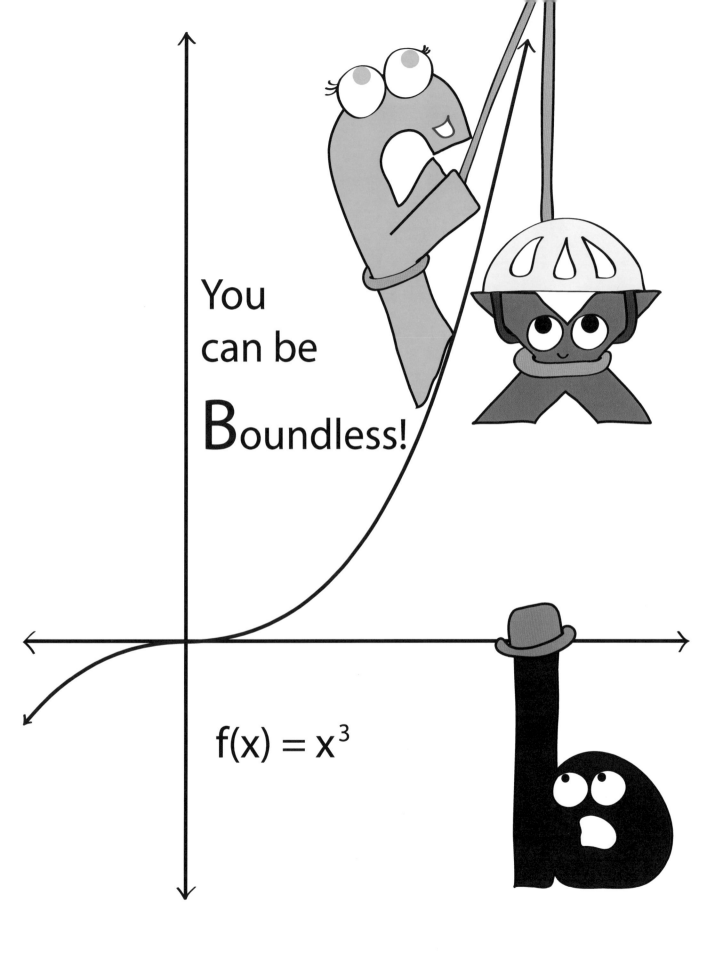

You can be Convex or Concave!

$$f(x) = -\sqrt{r^2 - x^2} + r$$

You can have a Derivative!

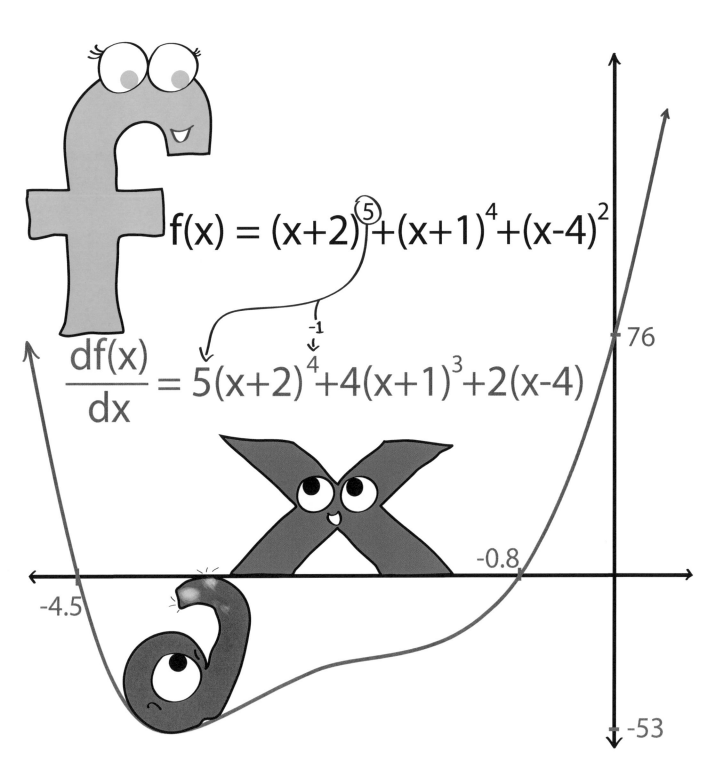

$$f(x) = (x+2)^5 + (x+1)^4 + (x-4)^2$$

$$\frac{df(x)}{dx} = 5(x+2)^4 + 4(x+1)^3 + 2(x-4)$$

Look how Functional we are together!

You can have Global extrema!

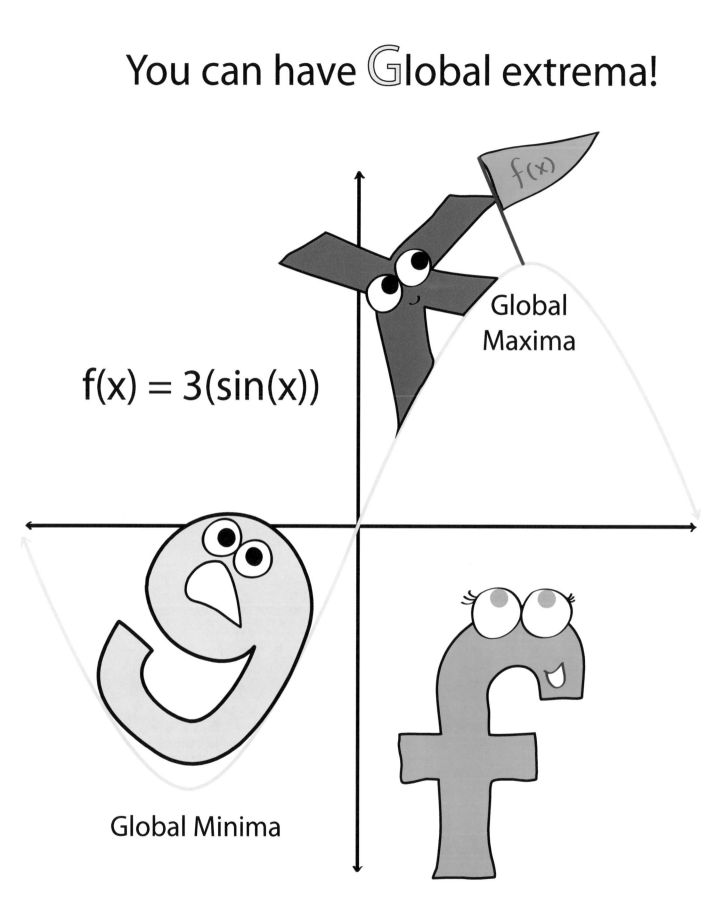

$f(x) = 3(\sin(x))$

Global Maxima

Global Minima

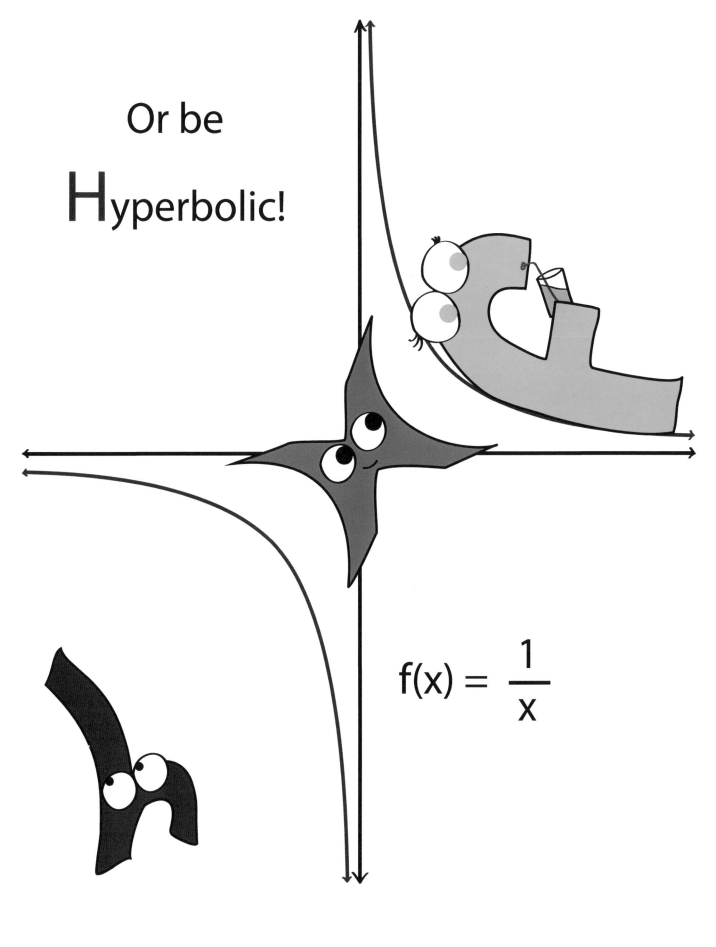

You can be Irregular...

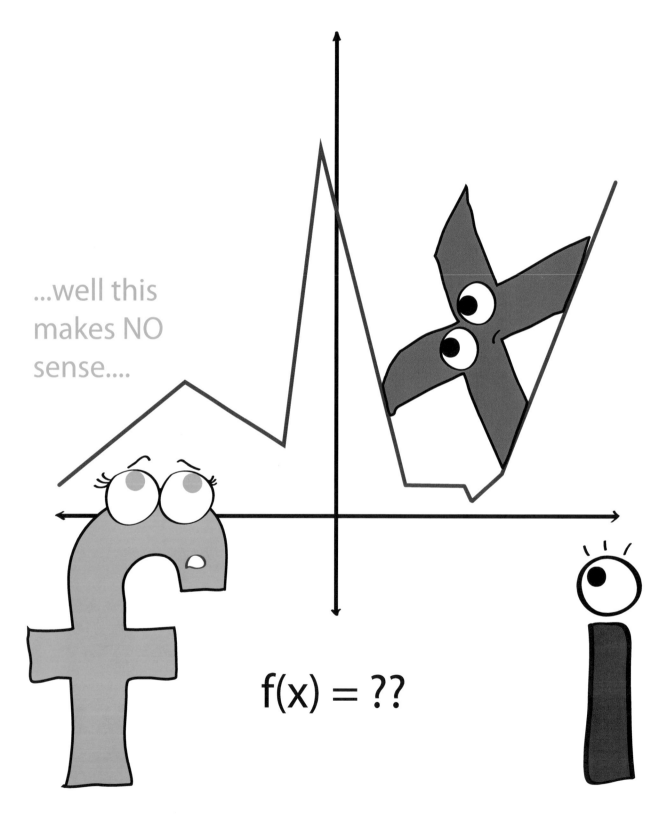

You can Jump from one spot to the next!

$$f(x) = \begin{cases} 3 & \text{if } x < 1 \\ 1 & \text{if } x > 1 \end{cases}$$

You can be the

King of Knowledge!

if 0<x<5:

$$f(x) = -\left(x - \frac{(0+5)}{2}\right)^2 + \frac{(5-0)^2}{4}$$

else:

$$f(x) = 10 \quad \text{if } \lceil x \rceil = \text{even}$$
$$f(x) = 9 \quad \text{if } \lceil x \rceil = \text{odd}$$

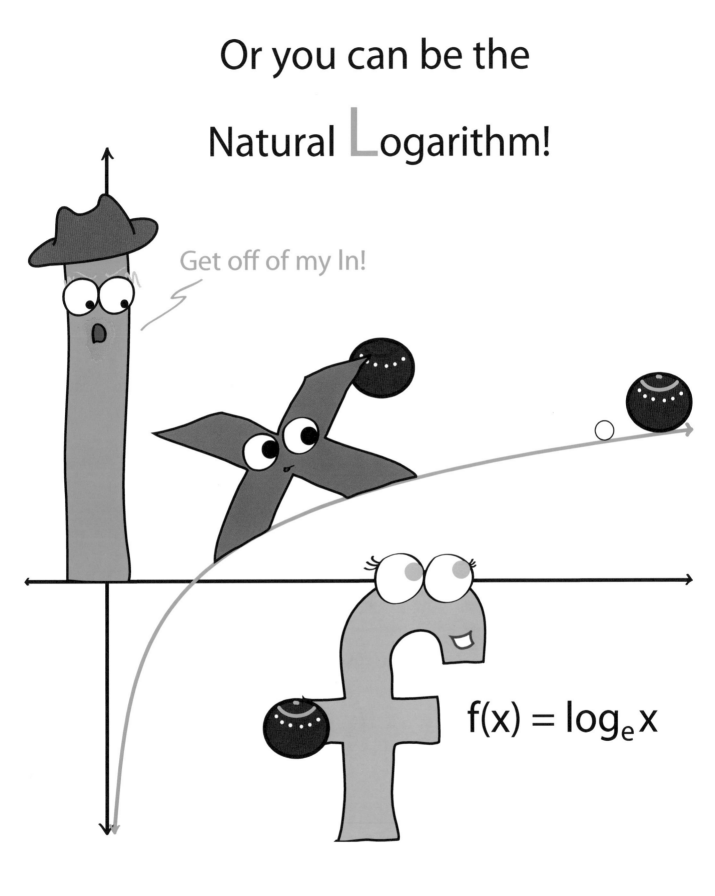

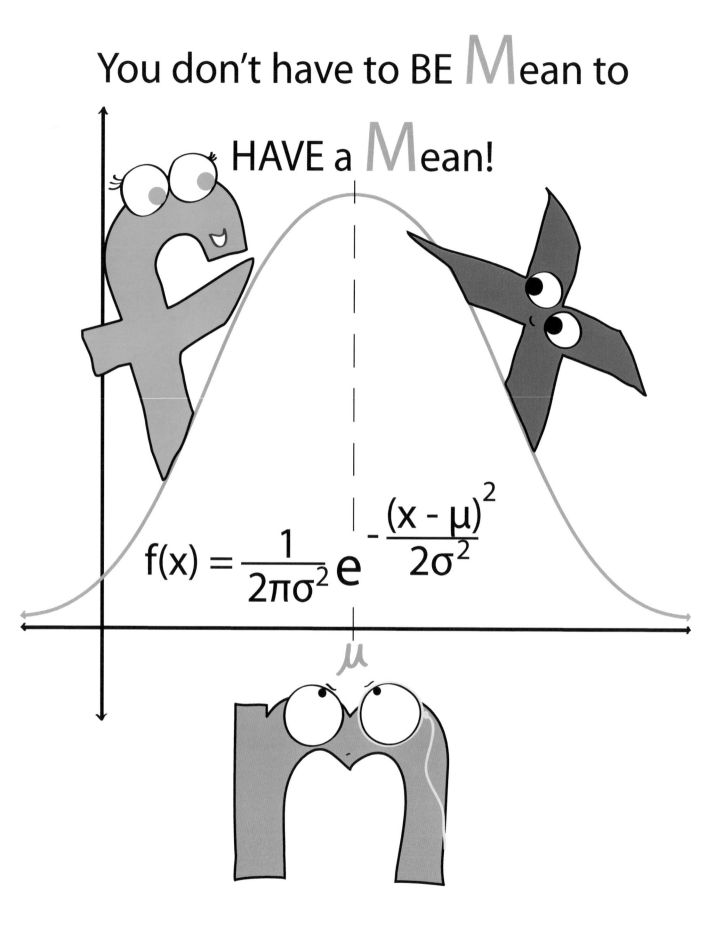

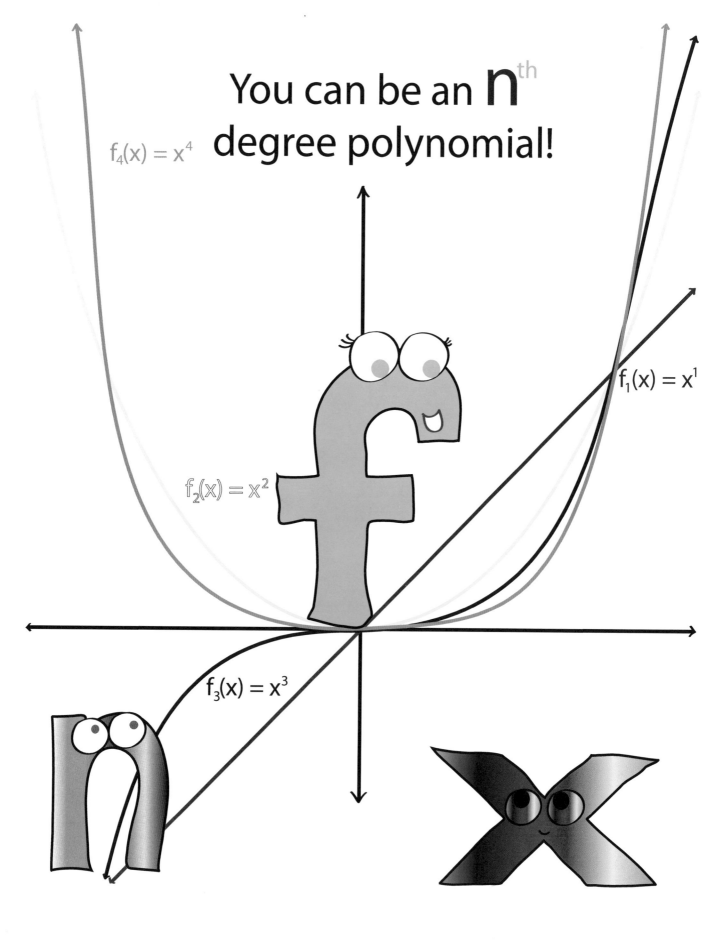

You can be ⓞne-to-ⓞne!

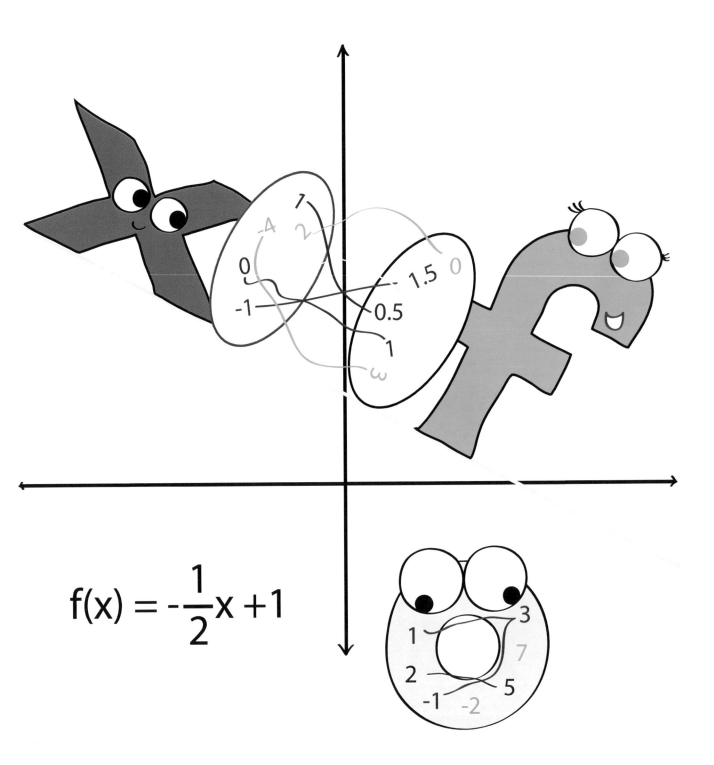

$$f(x) = -\frac{1}{2}x + 1$$

Or you can be a Parabola!

$f(x) = x^2$

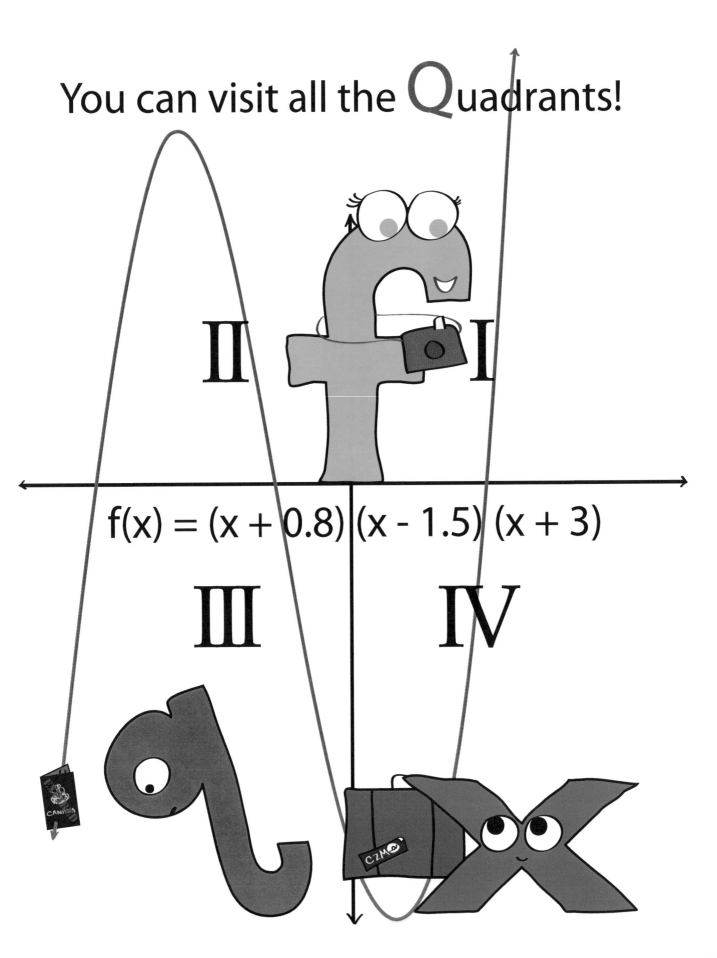

You can visit all the Quadrants!

II   I

f(x) = (x + 0.8) (x - 1.5) (x + 3)

III   IV

You can model Regression!

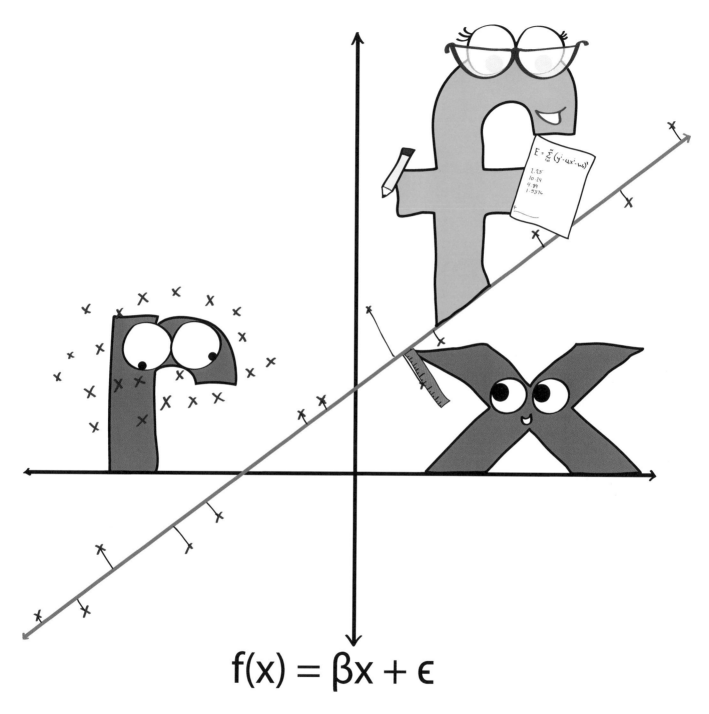

$$f(x) = \beta x + \epsilon$$

You can have a Slope!

$$f(x) = mx + b$$

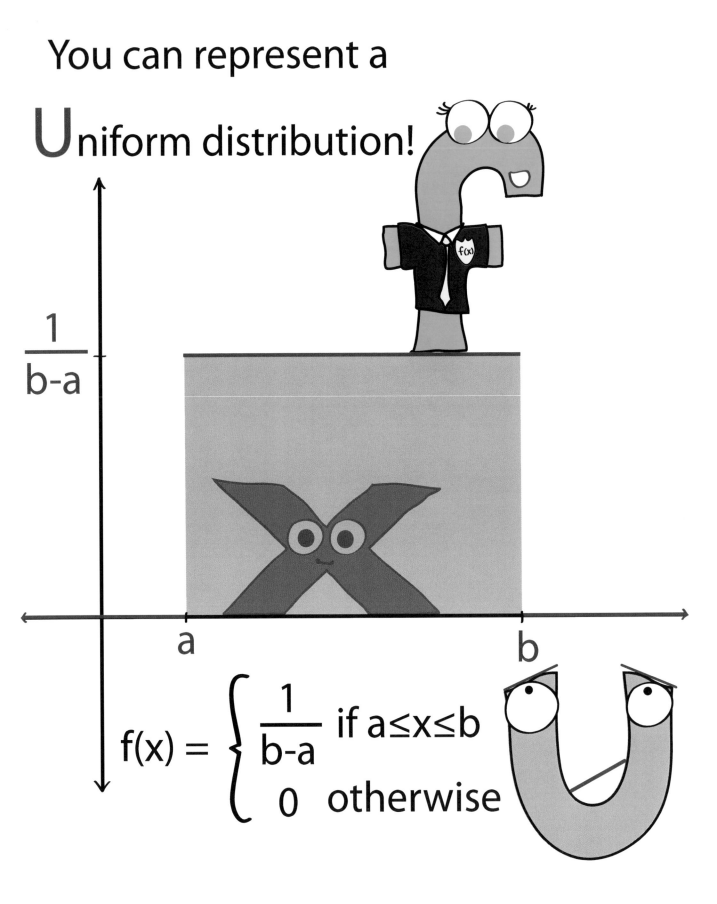

And you'll always pass the Vertical line test!

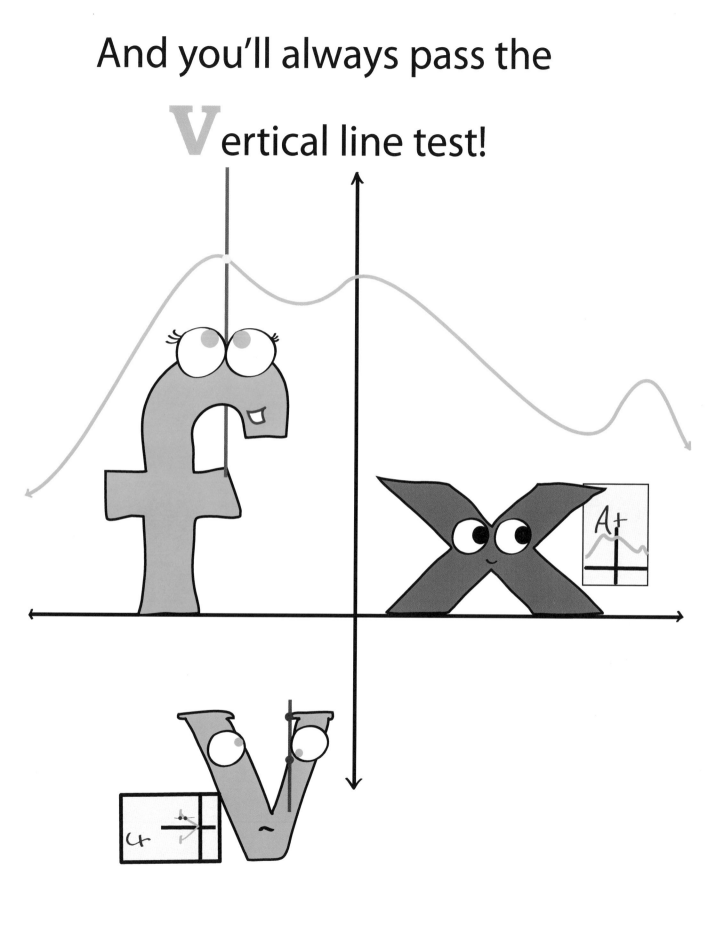

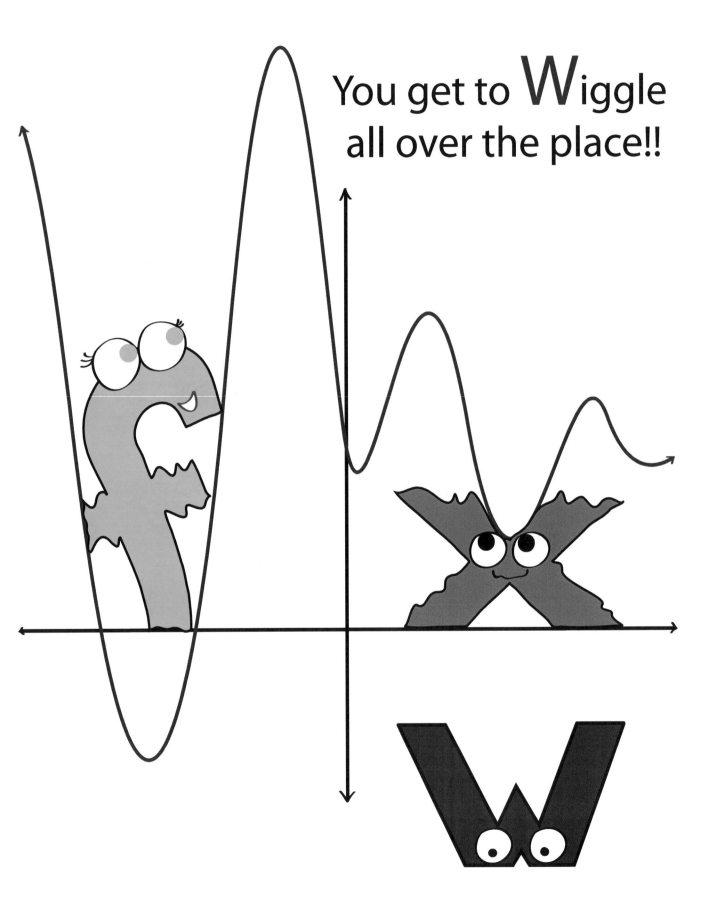

You can always be yourself!
f(x) = x

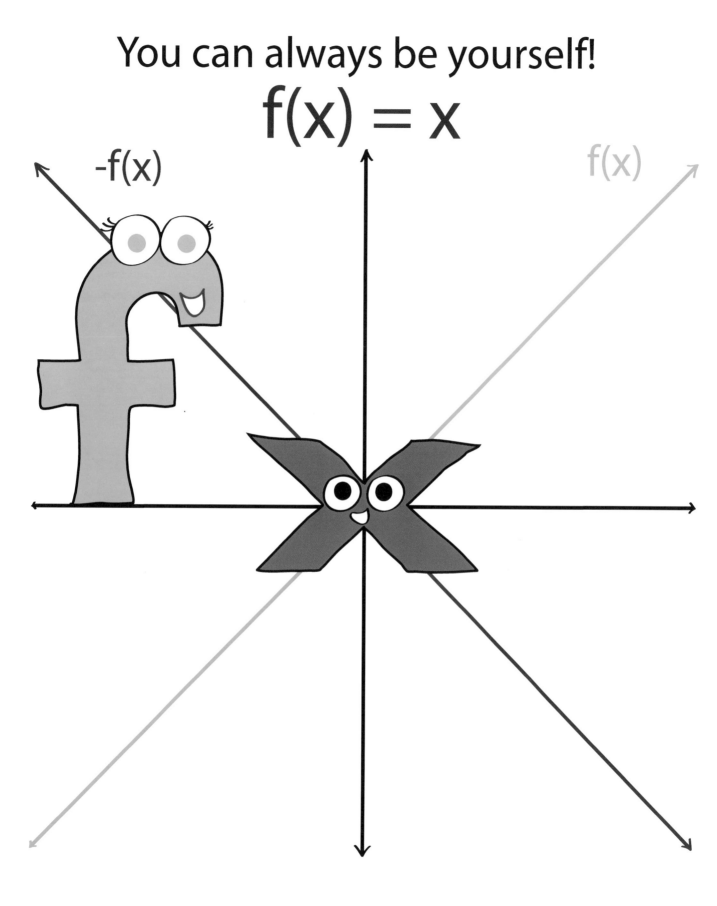

You can intercept Y!

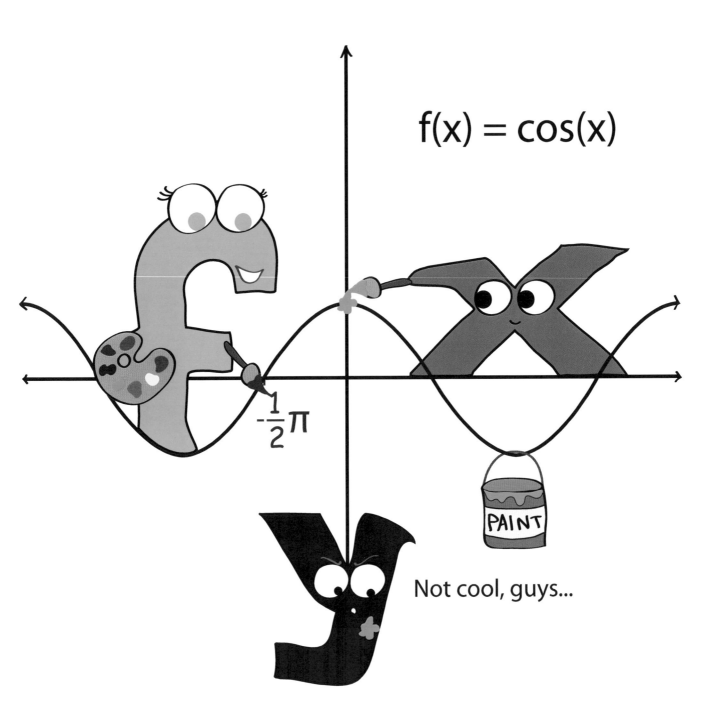

$f(x) = \cos(x)$

$-\frac{1}{2}\pi$

Not cool, guys...

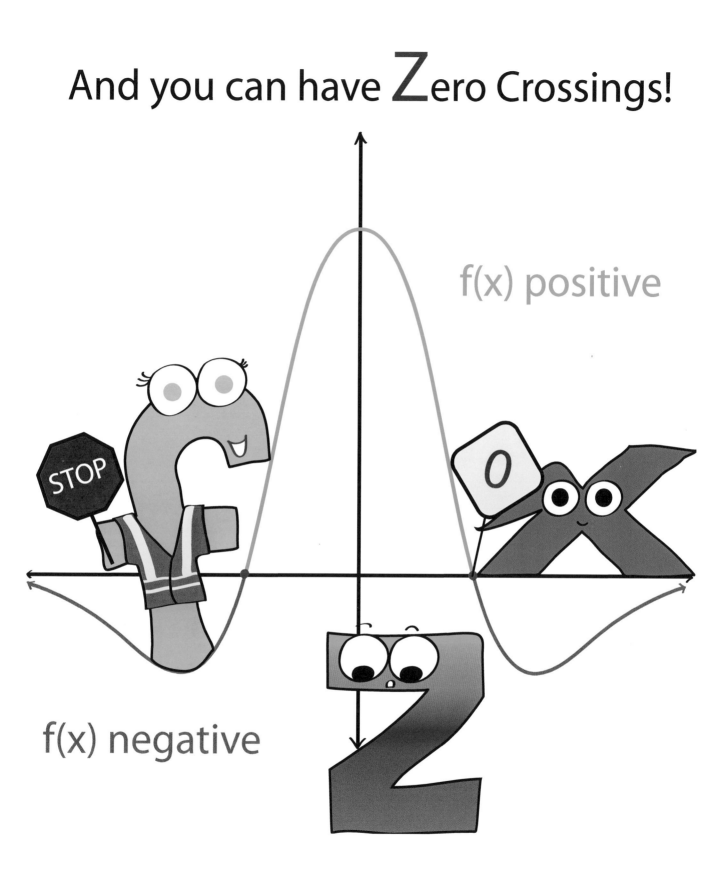

Wow! I CAN be anything!
You're my best friend, f!

Yay! Let's draw
Gaussians together!

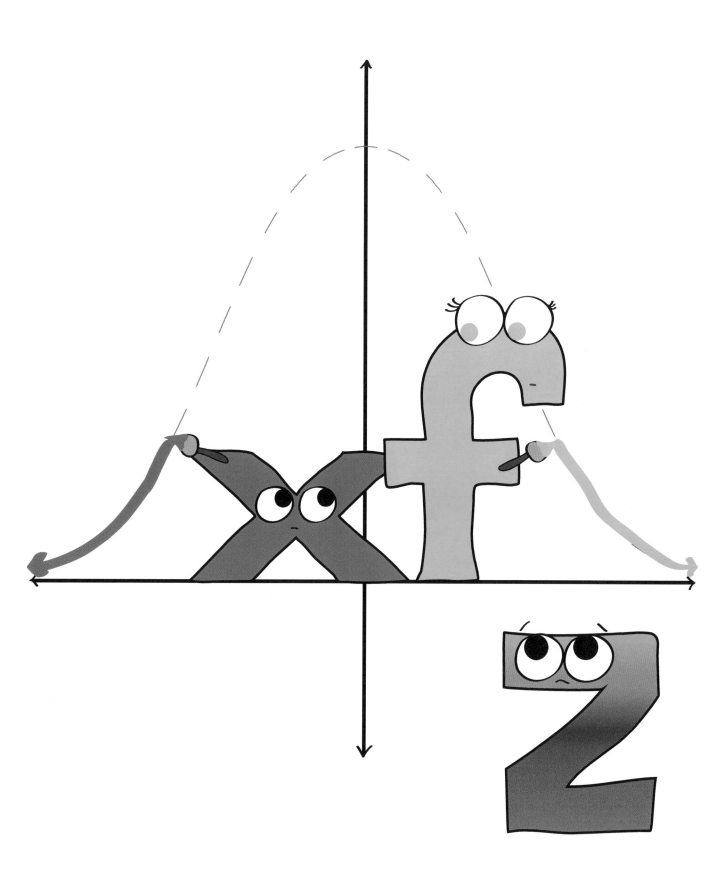

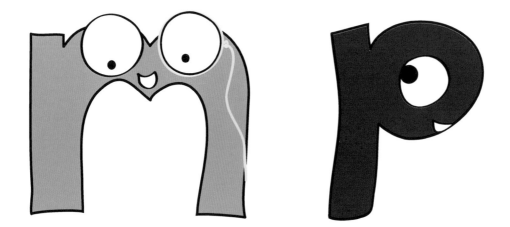

We can have Multiple Parameters!

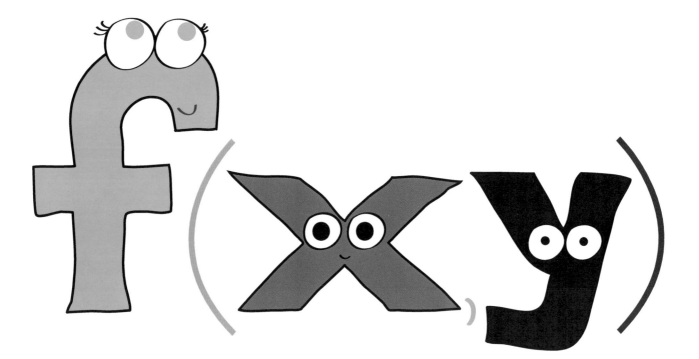

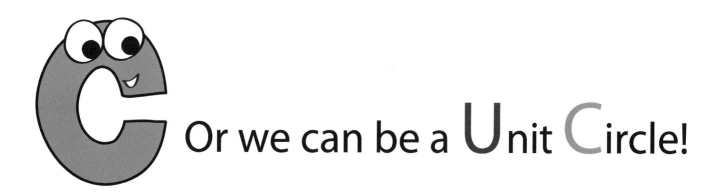

Or we can be a Unit Circle!

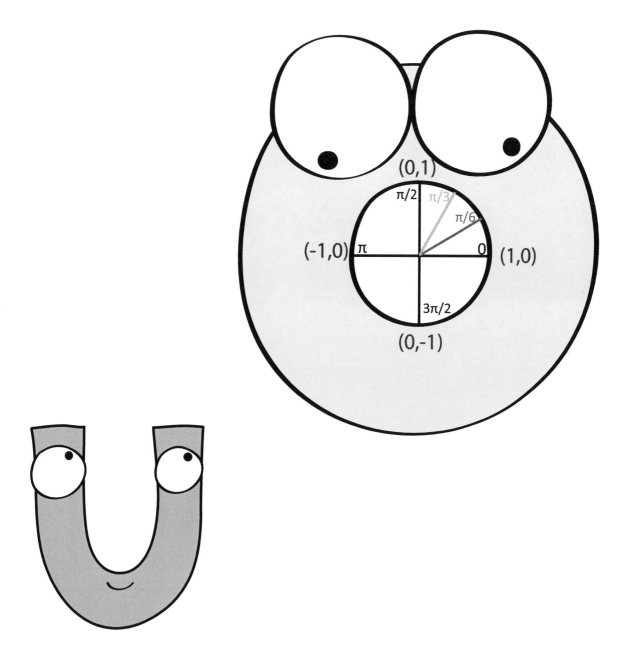

And all the letters saw that x really could be anything... including a great friend.

Special Thanks to:

Jonathan Schmidt – for proofreading the mathiness and letting me
use his graphing calculator, a TI-92 which he frequently refers to as God.

David Schmidt – for additional proofreading of mathiness.

Daniel M.T. Wood – for perfectly capturing my likeness.

All of the Computer Science and Math professors at
the University of British Columbia
and
the University of Victoria

and to:

Sarah Inouye – for continuing to encourage delinquency in youths and adults.

References

Edwards, C. Henry, and David E. Penney, *Calculus: Early Transcendentals, Matrix Version* (6th ed.)
Upper Saddle River, New Jersey: Pretice Hall, 2002. p.237.

Stewart, James, *Multivariable Calculus* (6th ed.) California: Thomson Brooks/Cole, 2008. p. 1049.

Wikipedia (accessed May 2011):
http://en.wikipedia.org/wiki/Hyperbola
http://en.wikipedia.org/wiki/Linear_regression
http://en.wikipedia.org/wiki/Unit_circle

oMii by Daniel MT Wood

Omi M. Inouye is a gamer, a programmer, and an instigator. She recently obtained a B.Sc. in Computer Science from the University of British Columbia and doesn't quite know what to do next. She lives in New Westminster, BC with her fiancé, Jon, and their two cats.

She is an average math student.

Omi is also the author of *Andre Curse* and *A Girl's Guide to Dating a Geek*. For incoherent rants (not meant for children) or to contact Omi, please visit her website: www.omionline.ca

2762564R00031

Made in the USA
San Bernardino, CA
01 June 2013